KNOWLEDGE ENCYCLOPEDIA

LIGHT & ENERGY

Wonder House

(An imprint of Prakash Books)

contact@wonderhousebooks.com

ISBN : 9789354401688

Disclaimer: The information contained in this encyclopedia has been collated with inputs from subject experts. All information contained herein is true to the best of the Publisher's knowledge.

Table of Contents

LIGHTING UP THE WORLD

Light is what helps us see. It helps us distinguish objects, identify their shapes and colours, and note their movement. The biggest source of light is the Sun. Since Earth's rotation causes day and night, when sunlight reaches our part of the Earth, we experience daytime; and when we rotate away from the Sun, we experience nighttime.

The light of the Sun comes from nuclear reactions deep inside it. There are also other kinds of light, for instance, the lights we switch on at night. These devices give us light generated from electricity. When you light a candle, the light comes from the burning of the wick in air, which is a chemical reaction. The light of fireflies comes from another kind of reaction. The hot iron in an oven gives off light as a glow.

All of these things are different forms of energy—nuclear, electric, chemical, and thermal. Light, too, is energy. But what is energy? How is it measured? Can we make it? Can we destroy it? These are the questions that physicists ask themselves every day.

Energy is what makes our Universe the happening place it is. All the energy in our solar system came from the Sun, and continues to do so even today. Some of that energy was used over four billion years ago to create the rocky planet that we call home. Deep inside Earth, nuclear reactions make the core extremely hot and form the forces responsible for the Earth's rotation around its axis. Meanwhile, on the surface, plants take the energy from sunlight and turn it into **chemical energy** that is stored in food. When we eat the food, the energy gets transferred and is used to keep our bodies warm and provide us with the ability to run or walk or do any other activity. In the case of bats, birds, and some insects, it gives them the ability to fly. Also, much of the heat that we derive from burning coal, gas, or wood is still the energy that was produced by the Sun and trapped by ancient plants millions of years ago.

So, let's explore the fascinating world of energy and light in the next few pages.

▶ *The Sun is the source of all energy on our planet, directly or indirectly*

Photons

Sunrise; when a tiny bit of Earth comes face to face with the Sun, as our planet rotates, birds begin to chirp, and alarms begin to go off in our homes. Everything is filled with light and a new day begins. But did you ever wonder what light really is? How does it travel so fast? How does it get to be all around us? And why are we so helpless without it?

For a very long time, people believed that light was an element of the Universe because all the light they had came from fire of some sort. For example, they saw the Sun, which gives us light during the day, as a great fireball, while the light they received at night came from lamps or logs of burning wood. Over time, scientists did experiments and theorised that light was some form of wave, that moved through an invisible substance (called ether) in space, just as waves move on the surface of the sea. Later, various experiments highlighted that light is actually made of tiny particles. These particles are called photons and have no weight at all, but have energy that can be measured. Today, several scientists believe that light is both a wave and a particle at the same time. This is called wave-particle duality.

◀ *Nuclear fusion reactions deep inside stars are the source of all the photons in our Universe*

The Speed of Light

The speed of photons travelling in a vacuum is 2,99,792 kilometres per second. As photons are massless, nothing heavier can travel faster than them. However, light does slow down when it enters a gas, liquid, or solid, where it interacts with the electrons of the material. The speed of light is 2,25,000 kilometres per second in water and 2,00,000 kilometres per second in glass.

★ Incredible Individuals

At college, Max Planck wanted to choose physics, but his professor told him that it would be futile as all the major discoveries had been made. Planck went on to study physics anyway, and ended up changing it forever with the quantum theory.

▲ *We can see objects because particles of light called 'photons' are reflected off them and enter our eyes, where they are captured by special 'vision' cells*

Quantum Theory

In 1900, the German scientist Max Planck suggested that all energy existed in fixed units called quanta. The more quanta of energy a substance has, the more energy it possesses, either as electricity, heat, light, or magnetism. For example, each quantum of electrical energy is called an electron. The more electrons a wire has, the more current it carries.

For his theory, Planck won the Nobel Prize in Physics in 1918. But what about other forms of energy such as light? In 1905, the Swiss scientist Albert Einstein suggested that light, too, is made of tiny quanta (now called photons). The more photons in a beam of light, the brighter it is. He theorised that not just energy, but even radiation itself was **quantised** in the same way.

Today, an entire field of physics called quantum theory studies how quanta of various kinds of energy behave, particularly photons. But not all photons are the same, for their energy depends on their frequency.

▲ Our modern understanding of light comes from Albert Einstein (second from left) and Max Planck (centre)

Wavelength and Frequency

Each photon 'oscillates' a number of times per second, even as it is moving forward in a beam of light. That means it travels some distance towards the left, returns to the centre, and then moves an equal distance to the right before coming back again to the centre and starting all over again. Imagine a ball tied on a string swinging sideways while you are walking forward. This vibration is called its frequency.

The frequency decides its **wavelength**, that is, the length it will travel forward for the duration of one complete vibration. The higher the frequency, the more energy the photon has, but its wavelength is shorter.

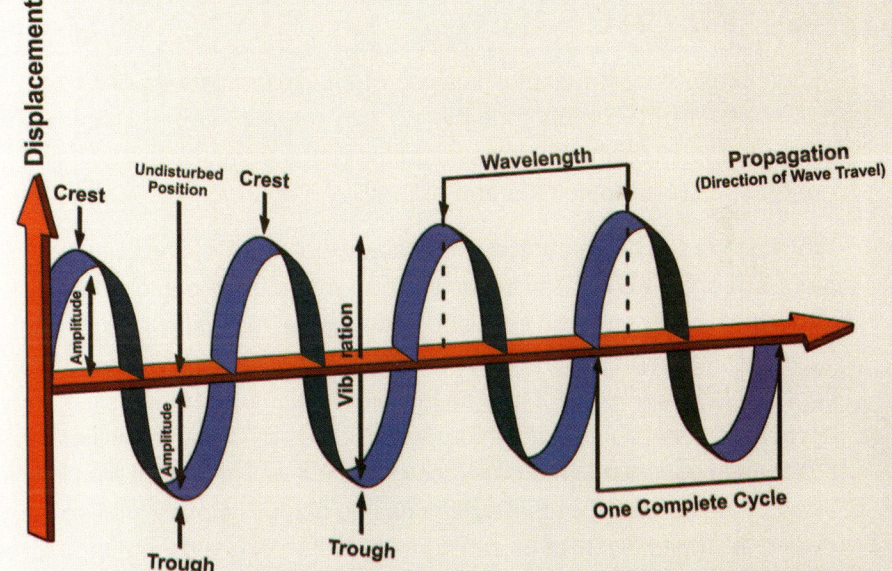

▲ Photons move as waves with a wavelength that decreases with energy

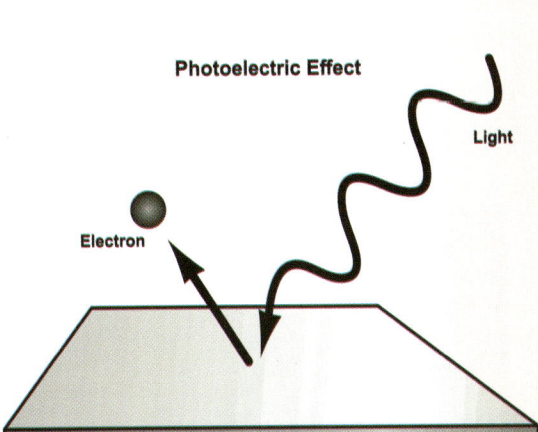

Photoelectric Effect

Light

Electron

Metallic Surface

The photoelectric effect is the emission of electrons or other free carriers when light is shone onto a material

▲ The photoelectric effect led to the discovery that light is made of photons

Photoelectric Effect

Many physicists knew that some materials, such as rubidium and caesium, discharge electrons when exposed to light, though they did not know why it happens. This is called the photoelectric effect. In 1905, Albert Einstein suggested that it could be possible only if light was made of something similar to electrons, but without an **electric charge**. He proposed that light is made up of photons, which are packets of energy. This theory not only solved the mystery of the photoelectric effect, but also won Einstein the Noble Prize in 1921.

Electromagnetism

Did you know that light is only one kind of wave? It belongs to a whole class of energy particles known as the electromagnetic (EM) spectrum. This contains all kinds of waves; from those whose wavelengths are in thousands of metres to those whose wavelengths are one-quadrillionth of a metre.

Electromagnetism happens when an electric charge moves through space, creating a magnetic field at right angles to it. This phenomenon was discovered by Michael Faraday and James Clerk Maxwell. When a charged particle moves as a wave, it sets up a waving magnetic field at a right angle to it. As a result, light was also seen to be an electromagnetic wave. Following this, Planck and Einstein established that the unit of electromagnetism was a photon.

Electric field
Magnetic field

▲ Electromagnetic waves are made of two distinct fields, electric and magnetic.

Visible Light

In quantum theory, the photon is a unit of **electromagnetic energy**, and not just light. The photons that we can see with our naked eyes are called visible light. Their wavelengths range from 380 to 750 nanometres (a nanometre is one-billionth of a metre).

Why can we see these photons? Actually, we cannot see the photons themselves, but we can see the object from where these photons originate. Our eyes have special rod cells and cone cells that are sensitive to different wavelengths of light. Each of these cells respond to a certain wavelength of light that hits it. When light falls on these cells, a tiny current passes from the cell to the optical nerve. The nerve collects the information from each cell and passes it to the brain, creating a picture in your head. The brain converts each wavelength of light into a different '**colour**'. This is what you 'see'. In reality, light has no natural colour. All these colours are the same in everyone's head, so all of us can agree that the sky is blue and the Moon is white.

👤 In Real Life

Some people lack some kinds of cells in their eyes, or have other genetic trouble, because of which they cannot see colour or differences in colour. Doctors call this **colour blindness**.

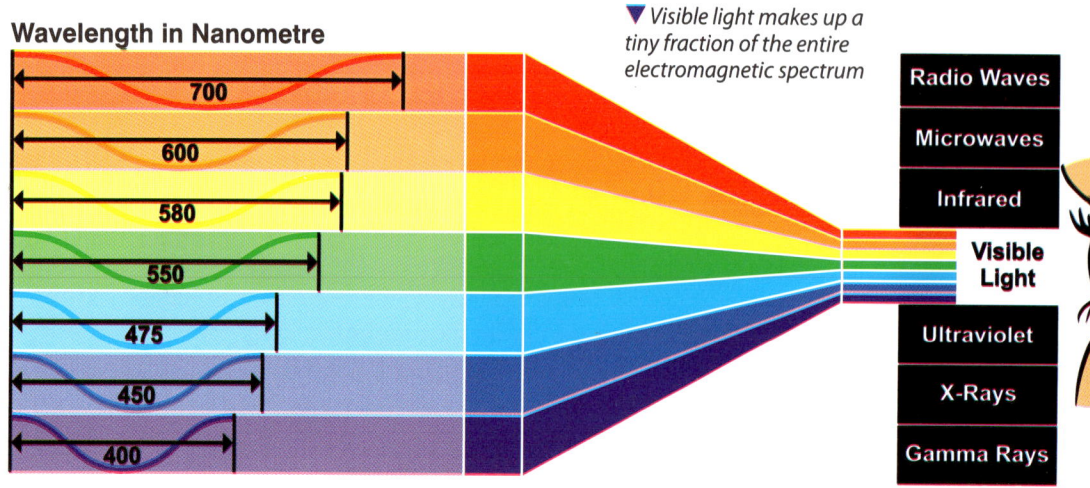

Wavelength in Nanometre

700
600
580
550
475
450
400

▼ Visible light makes up a tiny fraction of the entire electromagnetic spectrum

Radio Waves
Microwaves
Infrared
Visible Light
Ultraviolet
X-Rays
Gamma Rays

A magnetic scrap lifter

Other Waves

Our eyes cannot see most of the electromagnetic waves that exist in the Universe. But we can detect them in other ways, usually using a radio antenna or other specially made **detectors**. The photons whose wavelength is smaller than visible light make up ultraviolet (UV) light. Honeybees have cone cells, which they use to see UV photons. Photons with wavelengths smaller than UV rays are called **X-rays**, and those with even smaller wavelengths are called **gamma rays**. These photons have a lot of energy in them. When they hit an atom, they can remove electrons from it and turn it into a positively charged ion. Therefore, together they are called **ionising radiation**.

Waves with lengths higher than visible light are called **infrared (IR) waves**. They are used in night vision glasses. Waves with longer wavelengths than IR waves are **radio waves**. They don't have enough energy to remove electrons from atoms, so they are called **non-ionising radiation**.

Isn't It Amazing!

Ozone (triatomic oxygen or O^3) is a molecule that can absorb most ultraviolet radiation. It forms a covering above our atmosphere called the ozone layer, and stops UV rays from reaching us.

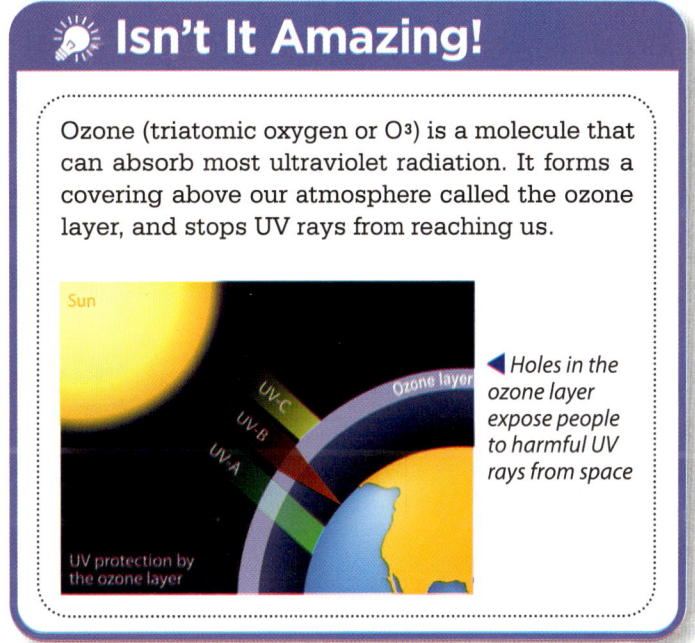

◄ *Holes in the ozone layer expose people to harmful UV rays from space*

Electromagnetic Spectrum

Radiation type	Radio	Microwave	Infrared	Visible	Ultraviolet	X-ray	Gamma ray
Wavelength (m)	10^3	10^{-2}	10^{-5}	0.5×10^{-6}	10^{-8}	10^{-10}	10^{-12}
Approximate Scale of Wavelength	Buildings	Humans	Honey bee	Needle point	Protozoans	Molecules	Atoms · Atomic nuclei

Frequency (Hz)

▲ *Photons with shorter wavelengths than visible light have higher energy, and those with longer wavelengths have lesser energy*

Energy

There are two laws that govern energy existing in the Universe. One of them, the Law of Conservation of Energy, says that energy can neither be destroyed nor created but can only be converted from one form to another. The other is the Law of Relativity, discovered by Albert Einstein, which dictates that energy can be converted into matter (and matter into energy). This is what happens deep inside the Sun, where four hydrogen atoms merge into one atom of helium and some of the matter is turned into energy in the form of photons of very high frequency. Scientists call this nuclear fusion.

Types of Energy

The Sun is the source of all the energy on our planet. Some of it is direct, like the light and heat that we get in daytime. Most of it is indirect, as we read earlier. But how many forms of energy are there, and how are they converted into each other?

Mechanical: This energy is visible in the movement of objects. We use this to do most of the work we want—from washing clothes in a machine, to running a blender or driving a car. There are two kinds of mechanical energy: kinetic energy that is present in moving things, and potential energy that is stored until needed. Sound is also a form of mechanical energy, which travels in the form of **mechanical waves** in the air.

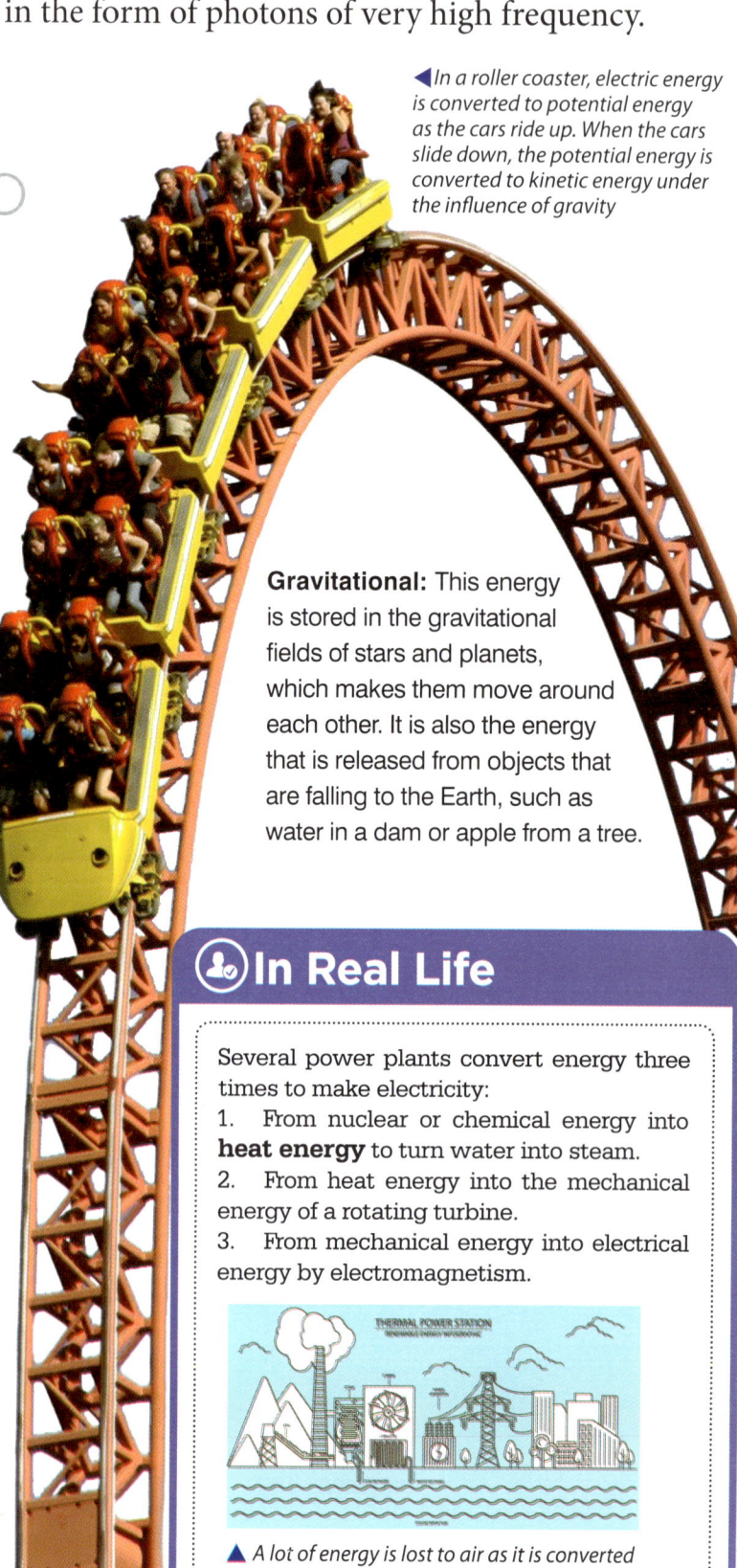

◄ In a roller coaster, electric energy is converted to potential energy as the cars ride up. When the cars slide down, the potential energy is converted to kinetic energy under the influence of gravity

Gravitational: This energy is stored in the gravitational fields of stars and planets, which makes them move around each other. It is also the energy that is released from objects that are falling to the Earth, such as water in a dam or apple from a tree.

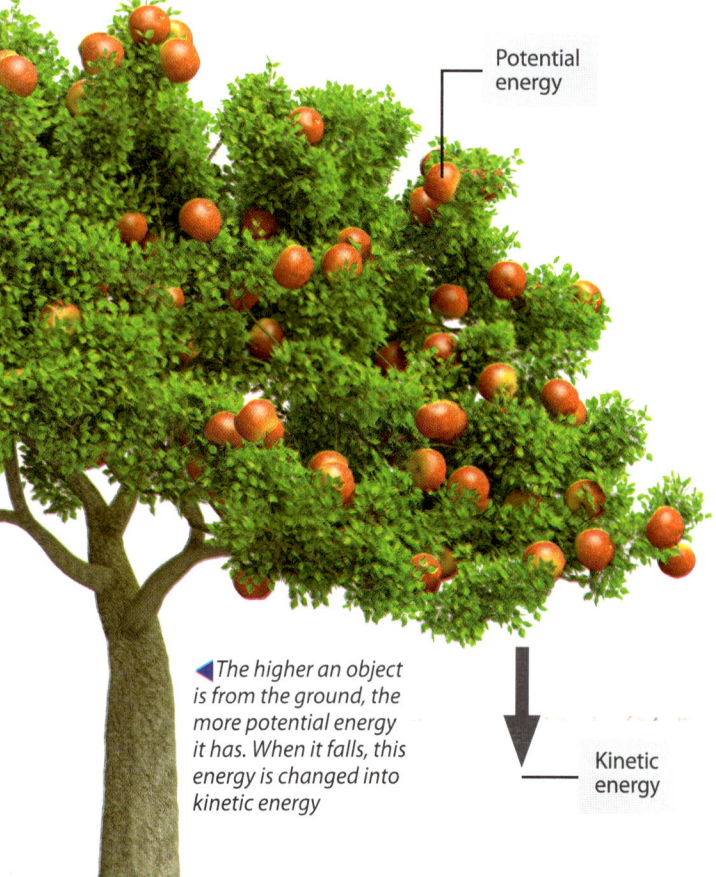

Potential energy

◄ The higher an object is from the ground, the more potential energy it has. When it falls, this energy is changed into kinetic energy

Kinetic energy

In Real Life

Several power plants convert energy three times to make electricity:
1. From nuclear or chemical energy into **heat energy** to turn water into steam.
2. From heat energy into the mechanical energy of a rotating turbine.
3. From mechanical energy into electrical energy by electromagnetism.

▲ A lot of energy is lost to air as it is converted from one form to another in a power plant

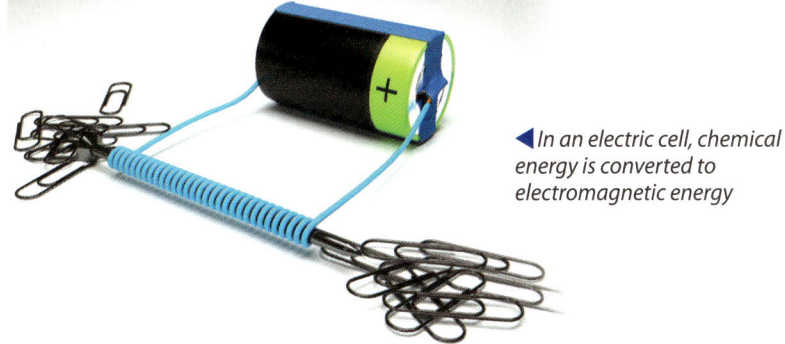

Electromagnetic: This energy is present in moving electric or magnetic fields, whether in a wire (electricity) or moving through space (radiation).

◄ *In an electric cell, chemical energy is converted to electromagnetic energy*

Thermal (Heat): This energy is stored in the vibrational movement of atoms, so it is really a form of mechanical energy, but at the atomic level. When a material is heated, the atoms vibrate faster and push each other away. This makes the material expand. When the material loses heat, the atoms vibrate less and therefore come closer. This is called contraction.

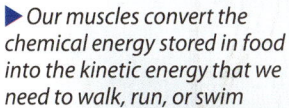

► *A matchstick converts the chemical energy stored in its head into thermal energy when it is struck*

Chemical: This energy is stored in chemical bonds between atoms. It is the energy that we get from food which is saved in our bodies. It is also the energy stored in fossil fuels such as coal, petroleum, and natural gas.

► *Our muscles convert the chemical energy stored in food into the kinetic energy that we need to walk, run, or swim*

Nuclear: This energy exists in the nuclei of atoms. When an atom is split into two in a nuclear reactor, this energy is released.

💡 Isn't It Amazing!

Our Universe is a giant sphere, which is expanding. The galaxies at the edge are accelerating away from each other faster than those at the centre. Explaining this phenomenon, scientists proposed that there might be other forms of energy that we know nothing about. Since we cannot measure them, these forms of energy are called dark energy. Our Universe is made up of 68% of dark energy and about 27% is dark matter.

▲ *Dark energy might push galaxies away from each other but it does not seem to affect anything on Earth*

Radiation

Why can energy be converted from one form to another? Most of it has to do with photons. When photons of certain wavelengths hit certain kinds of atoms, such as metals or semiconductors, they knock off electrons. This is seen in our lives in two very different ways:

1. Light from the Sun is turned into electricity in a photovoltaic cell. If you connect such cells to an electrical circuit, you can get an electric current.

2. Radio waves can move electrons which are loosely bound to metal surfaces to create a small current which is proportional to their wavelength. This principle is used in making antennas for radios.

When photons hit most other kinds of atoms, the energy of the photon is absorbed. The atom becomes excited and vibrates faster, thus becoming 'hot'.

When a nucleus explodes (fission), it releases its energy in photons. When a substance burns, it releases some energy as heat (vibrating molecules) and some as light (photons), and that's why you see a flame. Both of these kinds of energy are called radiation.

◀ *Electric devices work by converting electrical energy into other forms*

 ## Incandescence

Have you seen iron glow when it is heated in a forge? That's because iron, like other metals, emits light when heated at an extremely high temperature. The atoms absorb the energy from heat and then give it out as photons. This is called incandescence. In an incandescent lamp, electricity is used to create heat in a metal filament.

▲ *Incandescent lamps are either filled with inert gas or vacuumed to prevent the filament from corroding*

Fluorescence

In certain materials, when photons fall on their atoms, the electrons in the atoms absorb the photons. Such materials are called phosphors. The electrons then become 'excited', but after some time they release the extra energy and return to their normal state. This released energy is emitted as another photon, but this photon has a lower frequency (higher wavelength) and therefore lesser energy than the original. This is called fluorescence. It is seen best when materials absorb UV light and emit visible light.

In a fluorescent lamp, electricity makes an incandescent filament emit UV light. This falls on a phosphor coating that lines the inner side of the bulb. The phosphor absorbs the UV light and emits bright white light.

▲ *Both incandescent and fluorescent lights are now being replaced by LED lights*

Radio Waves

Radio waves are used for communication all over the world. These are waves of long wavelengths having low energy. They are emitted from a transmitter based on Earth which converts electrical signals into electromagnetic waves. These waves are received by satellites in space, which then transmit them back to Earth at a different wavelength. Some radio waves don't need satellites but are instead reflected by ions present in the ionosphere, part of the upper atmosphere.

In Real Life

Some types of metals absorb light in the X-ray spectrum (0.01 to 10 nanometre wavelengths) and emit it in the spectrum of visible light. Each metal has specific wavelengths at which it emits light, this is called its emission spectrum. This property can be used to find out what metals a material is made of.

Gamma Rays

Gamma rays are photons of extremely high energy. These are emitted during nuclear reactions and are highly dangerous. They remove electrons from every atom in their path, turning them into ions. Nevertheless, they can be used in irradiation, a procedure in which they are used to kill infectious bacteria or cancer cells.

◀ *Gamma rays are also emitted by black holes and stars known as quasars*

Optics

Did you know that the person you see in the mirror is not you but a slightly modified version of you? Because the right hand of the person in the mirror is actually your left hand and your right hand is your reflection's left hand; this is called a lateral inversion. But before we race on to that, let us understand something about reflection, refraction, and diffraction, which make up a fascinating field called Optics. This is a field whose scientific history begins with Isaac Newton, though, unlike his study of gravity, there were no apples harmed in the process.

Reflection

We've read earlier that light behaves both as a particle as well as a wave (pages 4–5). Well, if it behaves like a particle, then it should bounce like a ball when it hits a hard surface. That's exactly what happens when light is reflected on a mirror or a shiny surface. Shine is a property of metals that have loose electrons. These electrons keep photons from passing into the metal and reflect them instead. At whatever angle the photons hit the reflector, they travel away from it at the same angle. That's why when you turn a mirror, the reflection seems to move away by an opposite angle.

Absorption

Surfaces that are not very shiny, such as a cotton cloth, garden soil, and so on, will absorb light. Some photons of incoming light give up their energy to the electrons of the material they hit. You know that the energy of a photon depends on its wavelength. Each material absorbs photons of a certain wavelength and reflects the rest. The wavelength of photons reflected gives you the colour of the absorbing object. So, an object is blue if it absorbs photons of all colours but blue (that is, the range of light waves with wavelengths between 450 and 495 nanometres).

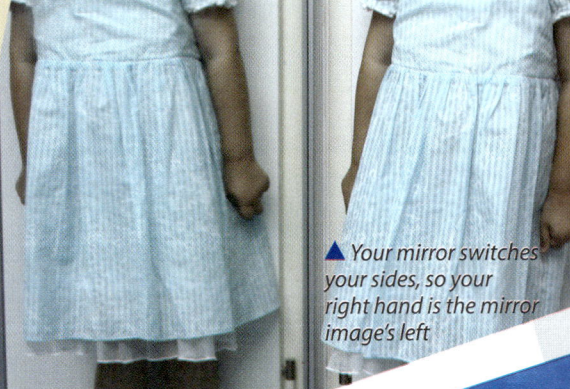

▲ *Your mirror switches your sides, so your right hand is the mirror image's left*

▼ *The sea looks blue because it transmits most wavelengths except blue, which it reflects*

💡 Isn't It Amazing!

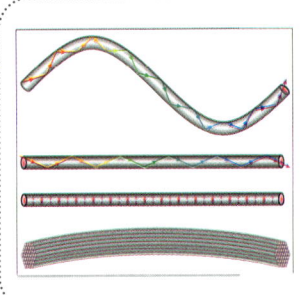

If light enters a tube whose inner surface is mirrored, the light will undergo multiple reflections until it comes out at the other end of the tube. This is called total internal reflection. This is the idea behind optical fibres, which convert computer signals (such as an email you wrote) into light rays of different wavelengths. The signals can travel at the speed of light to reach the destination.

◄ *Total internal reflection in optical fibre cables*

Transmission

Some objects, such as water and glass, neither reflect light nor absorb it. They transmit the light instead and are hence called transparent. Some objects, such as frosted glass, absorb some light and transmit the rest. These are called translucent. Objects that do not transmit any light at all are called opaque.

▼ *Water (left) is transparent, while lemonade (right) is translucent*

▼ *Refraction makes a pencil look out of shape under water*

In Real Life

Stellar spectroscopy is the study of the spectra of starlight, that uses a special machine that looks at the wavelengths of lights coming from a star. While the spectrum of any star emits most of the wavelengths of visible light, it shows some black lines, which correspond to the light the star has absorbed (called its absorption spectrum). These lines, called Fraunhofer lines, first observed in 1802, tell you what elements the star is made of.

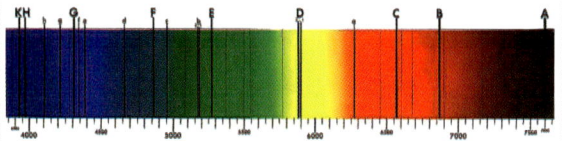

▲ *The depth of the lines indicate temperature, and the wavelength shifts point to motion of the composite gases*

Refraction

When you get into the bathtub, do you wonder why your body suddenly looks out of shape? Or why things look bigger or smaller when you look through mum's or dad's glasses? That's because water and glass bend light. When light travelling through air enters a denser medium, it loses speed, as the photons encounter resistance from the material's electrons. The speed of light in water is three-fourths its speed in air. This also causes a change in the angle of light which physicists call refraction. Refraction is used to build contact lenses that correct eyesight.

▼ *Soap bubbles diffract white light into its many colours*

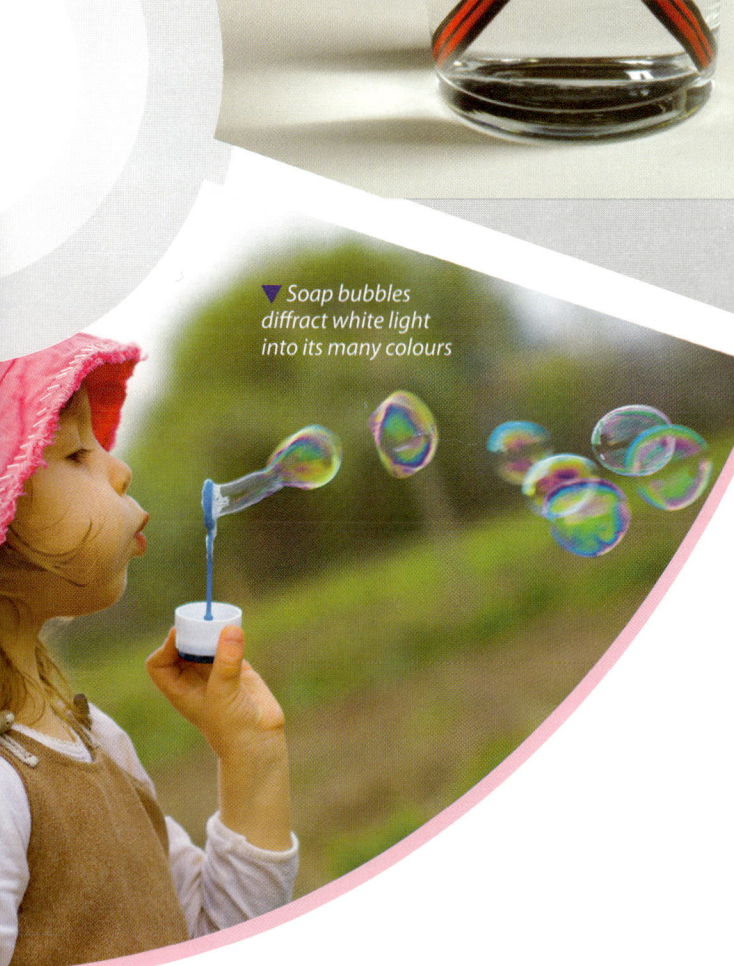

Diffraction

Ever blown soap bubbles and seen rainbow colours when light shines on them? That's because the bubbles diffract light. Diffraction happens when white light (that is light of all wavelengths) is refracted by a medium (like glass or water). As the photons slow down, they travel at different speeds according to their energy, so they bend at different angles. This means that photons of different wavelengths (colours) get separated.

Different crystalline solids will diffract light in different patterns. These patterns of diffraction are used by scientists to figure out the chemical composition of a substance.

Reflection

According to an ancient Greek legend, Medusa was a monster who could turn you to stone if you looked at her. Perseus was a Greek hero who was sent to kill her while she was asleep. To avoid looking at her, he used a mirrored shield to get closer to her and defeat her. As this legend is about 4,000 years old, we know that mirrors were known as far back as then.

Mirrors are one way in which humans use the science of optics (how light behaves with different media). Two other devices that have been with us since ancient times are the lens and the prism. Here we will look at how these devices work. Sometimes these are directly useful, while other times they are part of other devices like **telescopes** and cameras, which combine many lenses and prisms.

▲ *An example of an ancient Chinese bronze mirror. The front would have been polished metal, and the back would have beautiful carvings*

🔍 Mirrors

A mirror is a surface that reflects light. Most mirrors known to us are made of glass, covered on one side by a coat of fine aluminium or silver dust. Other mirrors, used for astronomy, are often made of polished metal surfaces. Mirrors come in three types:

1. Planar: These are the most common ones, including dressing mirrors. The image in the mirror is laterally inverted, that is, right becomes left and left becomes right.

▼ *In a planar mirror, your left hand becomes your right hand, and vice versa*

2. Concave: The mirror is bowl-shaped, with the silvering on the outside. These mirrors are used to reflect incident light onto a single point (the focal point). They make an image look bigger, so dentists use them to examine your teeth.

▼ *Concave mirrors expand a small picture*

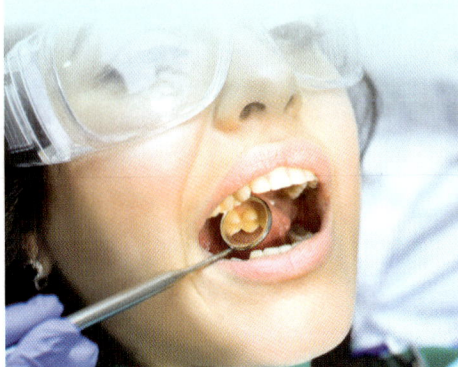

3. Convex: This mirror is also bowl-shaped, with the silvering on the inside. They make an image look smaller, so they can be used to condense a large field into a smaller space. That's why they are used in rear-view mirrors of cars.

▼ *Convex mirrors shrink a big picture*

Reflection by Mirrors

Here are some more things you should know about mirrors. The incident ray is the ray of light falling on the mirror, while the reflected ray is the ray of light that bounces off a mirror. The angle at which the ray of light meets the mirror is called the incident angle. You can try it yourself: Shine a flashlight onto a mirror in a dark room. As you change the angle at which the light meets the mirror, the angle of the reflected beam will change equally. This is called the angle of reflection.

Newtonian Telescope

While it was Galileo who invented the telescope, most telescopes today use a design made by Isaac Newton. The Newtonian telescope uses a concave mirror to focus the light coming from faraway stars onto a smaller flat mirror that then reflects the image into an eyepiece. The eyepiece may have lenses of different magnifications that allow you to see or photograph the star or other celestial bodies that you want to observe. These telescopes are very easy to build and are popular among astronomers.

▼ *How a Newtonian telescope works*

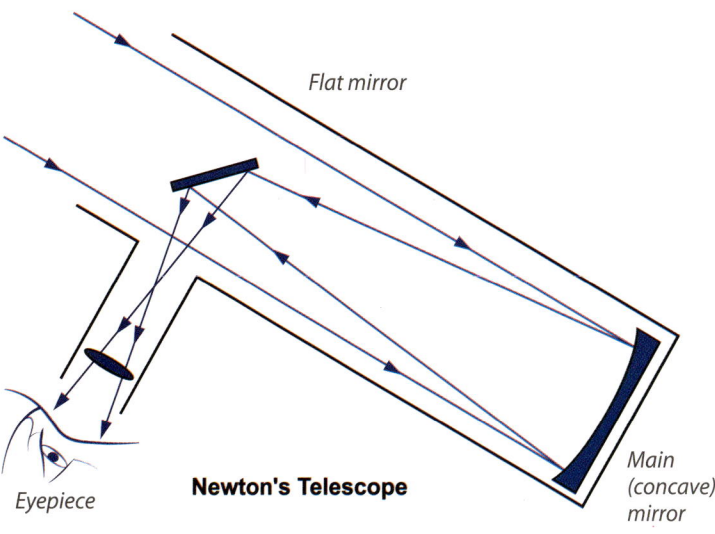

Flat mirror

Newton's Telescope

Eyepiece

Main (concave) mirror

⊙ Incredible Individuals

Archimedes, the ancient Greek scientist, is said to have used concave mirrors to defeat the invading Romans in the Battle of Syracuse in Italy (212 BCE). Some reports say that he used the mirror to focus the light of the Sun into an intense beam that burned the Roman ships. However, it is more likely that he used the blinding flashes of light to distract the soldiers instead.

◀ *A statue of Archimedes holding a concave mirror in modern Syracuse*

👍 In Real Life

In the Medieval Period, mirror-making was very expensive. The kings of France and Persia had halls of mirrors built in their palaces to show how rich they were. The walls of these halls are covered with mirrors of all kinds.

▲ *The Hall of Mirrors, Golestan Place, Tehran*

💡 Isn't It Amazing!

Charles Messier identified a list of 110 interesting objects in the sky, including galaxies, star clusters, and naebulae, during the late 18th century. Young astronomers use these objects to learn how to use a telescope.

◀ *The Messier Marathon happens every year on a new moon night in March, when astronomers try to observe all 110 Messier Objects*

Lenses and Prisms

A lens is a block of glass through which light is made to pass. Lenses can be concave or convex, though the latter is the most common. They use the power of refraction to make light either converge at a point (convex lenses) or diverge (concave lenses). A lens affects the view of an object behind it. Convex lenses are used in many instruments to focus light onto a point that needs to be lighted up, as well as in contact lenses and eyeglasses which help long-sighted people see better. In a camera, a **convex lens** shrinks the wide world into a small space. Concave lenses are used in flashlights and projectors to increase the area that can be lighted, and also in spectacles which help short-sighted people see better. In a movie projector, the **concave lens** does the reverse of the camera.

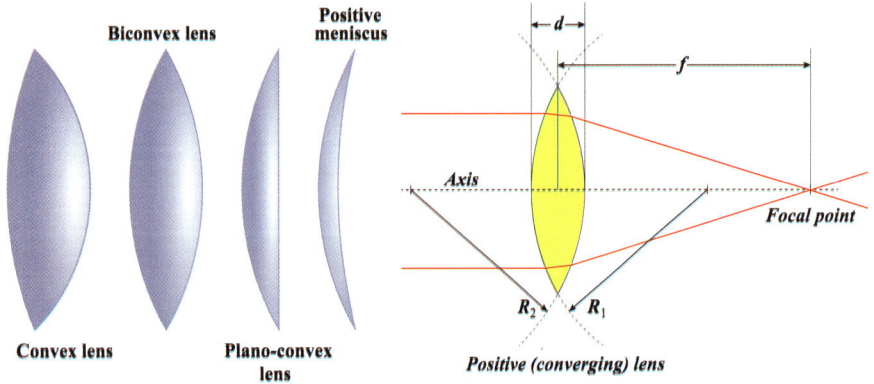

Convex & Concave Lenses

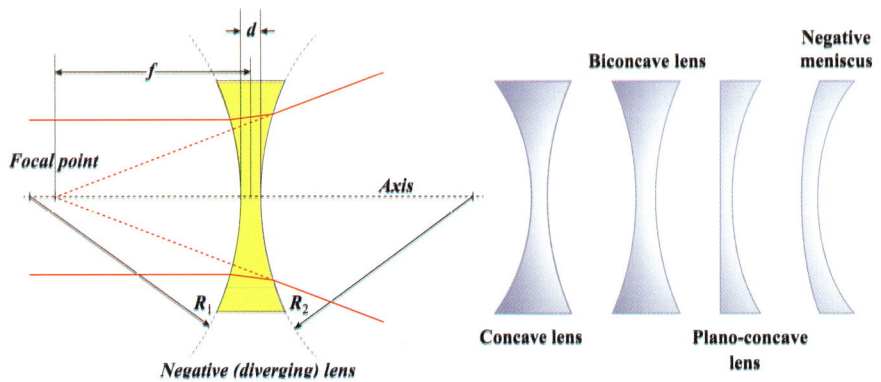

▲ Convex lenses focus light onto a focal point while concave lenses expand the area the light can cover

💡 Isn't It Amazing!

There is a lens in your eye too. It is made of transparent proteins and is known as the crystalline lens. But unlike a glass lens, the thickness of the eye lens can be increased or decreased, allowing you to focus on a faraway object or a near one. In some people, the ability of the lens becomes limited, due to which they need to wear glasses of the correct **power**.

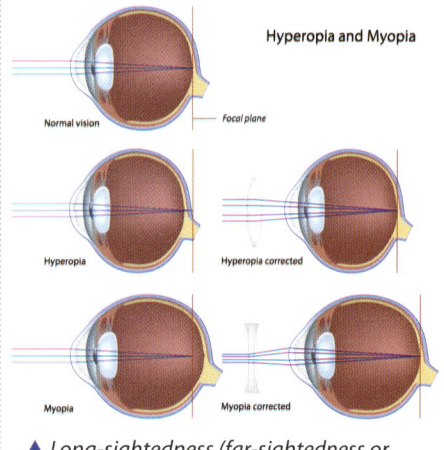

▲ Long-sightedness (far-sightedness or hyperopia) is corrected by convex lenses, while short-sightedness (near-sightedness or myopia) is corrected by concave lenses

Microscopes

The simplest microscope is a magnifying glass. It is a lens that is convex on both sides (**biconvex**), which projects light onto an object. As the light is reflected from the object, it comes back to your eyes in the form of an **image** which looks larger than it actually is. This is called **optical magnification**. If the image appears ten times larger than the object, it is said to be magnified 10 times.

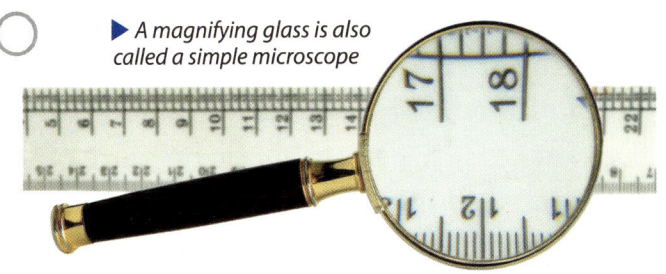

▶ *A magnifying glass is also called a simple microscope*

In a compound microscope, the idea is taken further by using more than one lens. A condenser lens collects light from outside (either sunlight or an electric light) and focuses it onto the object in the slide. As the light passes through the object, it falls on the first convex lens, which scientists call the 'objective'. This lens focuses the image onto the second lens, called the 'eyepiece'. This adds more magnification before the image reaches your eye. The thickness of the objective lens determines its **optical resolution**. High resolution means that the distance between the two objects the microscope can 'see' as separate ones is really small. Anything below the resolution will appear unclear. If the eyepiece magnification is more than that of the objective, you get empty magnification, that is, the image is larger but not better resolved.

◀ *Light from the condenser focused onto the objective lens of a microscope*

Prisms

A prism is a device that makes refraction happen twice. The first is when light waves enter from air into the prism, and the photons of different wavelengths separate. The second is when light leaves the prism back into the air, and the photons speed up again but are separated so much that they now exit as separate waves. Prisms are used together with light filters to get a beam of light of a single wavelength. They can also be used to turn a beam of light by an angle. This is the principle used in a submarine's **periscope**.

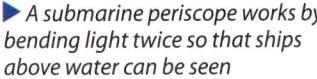

▶ *A submarine periscope works by bending light twice so that ships above water can be seen*

Changes of State

In Physics and Chemistry, a state or phase of matter is defined as the condition a substance is found in at any temperature or pressure. For example, at the atmospheric pressure of sea level, water is usually a liquid. If heated above 100°C, it boils and becomes a gas called steam. If steam is cooled below 100°C, it condenses back to water. This temperature is called the boiling/condensation point of water. If cooled below 0°C, water freezes and becomes a solid called ice. If ice is heated above this temperature, it melts. 0°C is therefore water's **freezing/melting point.** Sometimes, a solid turns directly to gas if heated fast enough. This is called sublimation.

▼ Ice can be transparent or near opaque depending on the level of impurities in the water

◄ Frozen carbon dioxide is called dry ice because at room temperature it sublimes directly from solid to gas

What Happens in a Phase Transition?

Think of water. In ice, the H_2O molecules have no freedom to move, except to vibrate a tiny bit about themselves. As you heat the ice, the heat is converted to kinetic energy and the molecules vibrate faster. When heated past 0°C, a sudden change occurs. The ice molecules now break free of the forces holding them and begin to move about with greater freedom. Nevertheless, they remain attracted to each other by weak **van der Waals forces.** Therefore, water still has a fixed volume.

When water is heated past its boiling point, it turns into steam. Any meagre force holding the molecules together is now broken completely and each molecule is on its own. Its kinetic energy makes it shoot about faster. If the steam is released into the atmosphere, it will disperse completely, as you see in a pressure cooker.

If the temperature drops, the kinetic energy is lost as heat. The molecules move around much less. When cooled below 100°C, the water molecules stick to each other and turn into droplets, which then begin to form puddles. If you cool these puddles below freezing point, the molecules begin to line up in rows and columns, turning into crystals of ice.

▼ Water is the most common liquid on our planet

▼ While mostly visible, saturated or super-heated steam is invisible

States of Matter

Solid

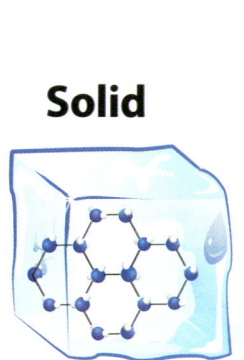

Gas

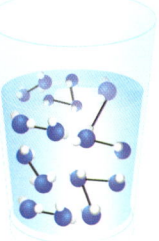

Liquid

◄ Changes of state are accompanied by changes in the movement of atoms or molecules

Latent Heat

Water does not start boiling the moment it reaches 100°C. Instead, some heat is absorbed without a change in temperature. This is called the latent heat of vaporisation. This heat is needed to break the hydrogen bonds that form between water molecules. Many other substances have their own specific latent heat of vaporisation.

Ice does not melt immediately at 0°C either. Instead, it takes some heat to break all the bonds between the atoms that hold them in the regular crystal structure of rows and columns. This is called water's latent heat of fusion. All crystalline substances have their own latent heat of fusion.

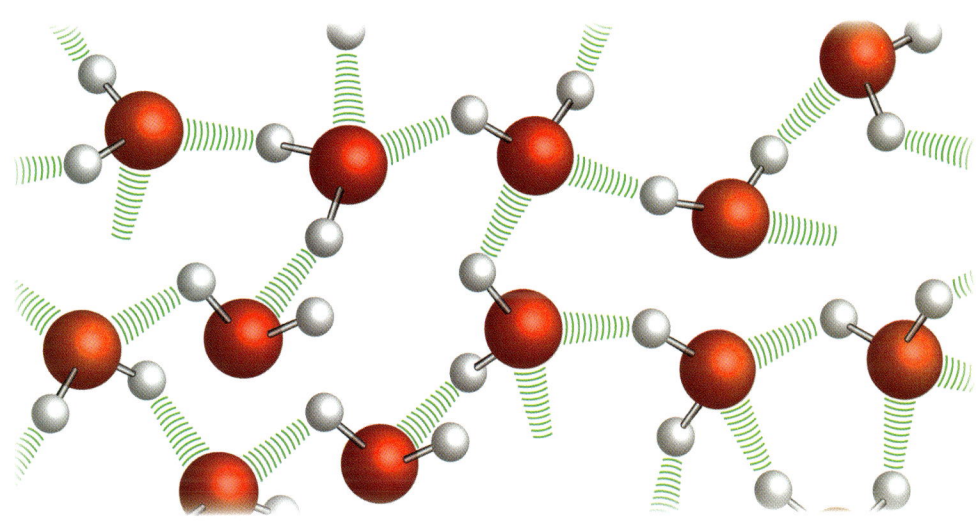

▲ *All hydrogen bonds between water molecules must be broken before it can boil*

Combustion

Not all things melt, boil, or sublime when heated. Some burst into flames instead. This is because when they are heated, they react with the oxygen in the air and undergo combustion. This is important for cooking oils, which need to be hot enough for frying, but not hot enough to start burning. The smoke point of an oil is the temperature at which it starts to smoke.

▶ *Heating oil beyond its smoke point may cause it to burst into flames*

Heat Transfer

Let's now turn our focus towards heat. Heat, as seen on page 9, is a form of energy that is stored in the movement of atoms and molecules. The hotter they are, the more kinetic energy they have. Because of this, heat can also travel and therefore make other things hot, because it moves from a place of high temperature to a place of lower temperature. If this did not happen, our Universe would be a cold dead place. Here we will look at how heat can be used to do a lot of our work.

▲ *Radiation is the method by which the Sun's heat is transmitted to our planet*

 ## Conduction

Ever wondered why a saucepan is stirred with a wooden spoon while cooking? That's because wood is a poor conductor of heat, that is, heat does not travel along the molecules of wood. On the other hand, it travels fast among the atoms of a metallic spoon, until the spoon becomes as hot as the sauce. This is called conduction of heat.

Metals have atoms arranged in neat rows and columns. When a metal atom gets heated, it begins to vibrate faster, converting heat into kinetic energy. As it vibrates, it crashes into the next atom, transferring some of the energy to it, so the next atom also begins to vibrate. In this way, all the atoms begin to vibrate, and the entire metal spoon becomes hot. Metals are therefore good conductors of heat. On the other hand, the molecules in wood are not arranged in a regular way at all and they all vibrate out of sync with each other. Hence, heat cannot travel in any one direction, and the spoon takes much longer to become hot.

▲ *A wooden ladle helps you stir chocolate while it melts without burning your hand*

Conduction

💡 Isn't It Amazing!

What happens if you put a flask with a shiny outer surface into one with a shiny inner surface and create a vacuum between them? There can be no heat transfer by conduction or convection, and the surfaces reflect the light, so radiation is also ruled out. This is the principle of the vacuum flask, which was invented by James Dewar.

Convection

Shell some peas and boil them in a saucepan. Do you notice that they bounce up and down as the water heats up? This is because of a form of heat transfer called convection, which occurs in liquids and gases. When water molecules are heated by the gas or electric coil at the bottom of the pan, they begin to move around faster and rise to the top. They push the colder water to the bottom, which then gets heated and moves up. This sets up a round motion in the water called a **convection current**. Convection currents allow for uniform heating and cooking of food in a pan or a steamer.

▲ Convection currents in a boiler make peas jump up and fall down

▼ The three different kinds of heat transfer

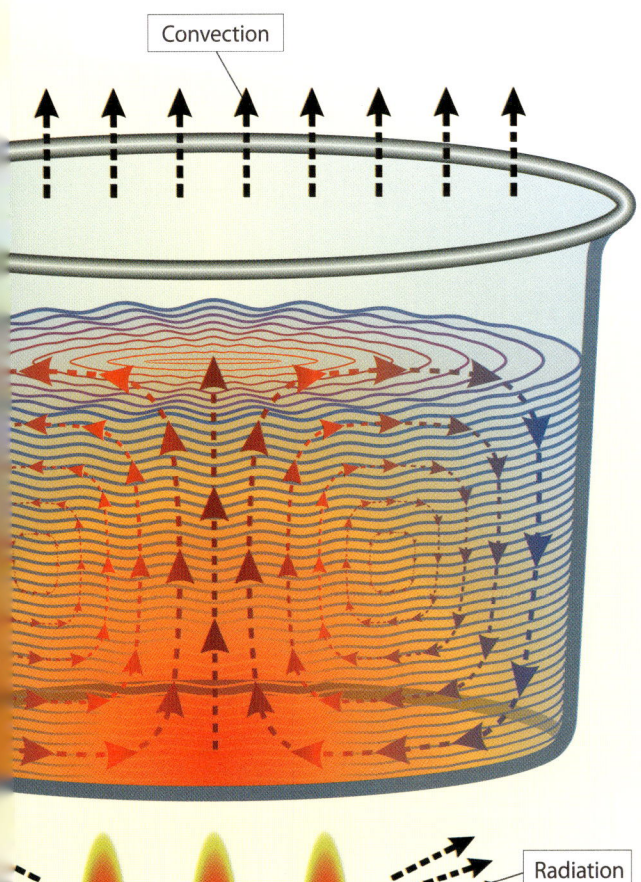

Convection

Radiation

Radiation

Radiation transfers heat even in a vacuum through photons whose energy is very high. In an electric radiator, which is used in many homes to heat rooms during winter, the electrons moving through the machine collide with the atoms it is made of, making them eject photons. These photons hit the molecules in the air and heat them, thus heating the room. Radiation is also how the Earth receives heat from the Sun.

▲ Radiators heat rooms in winters by converting electricity into electromagnetic waves

Energy and Work

In the 18th century, scientists realised that steam energy could be harnessed to do work. It is based on the principle that steam has a lot of kinetic energy when compressed, and that this energy can be harnessed to do useful work through a machine called an engine. Scientists tried to figure out how these engines could be made more **efficient**, so that they could get more work out of the energy put into them. In this process, the scientists discovered the science of **Thermodynamics**. But before we read further about this science, we need to learn a few definitions:

System: The set of molecules that one studies in thermodynamics. It can be a test tube full of liquid, or the whole Universe.

State: A description of a system that includes its temperature, pressure, amount of heat, and other physical properties.

Open System: A system which is open to the rest of the world, so both matter and energy can come in and go out. For example, water boiling in a vessel: energy goes from the stove to the water, but steam escapes into the air from the vessel.

Closed System: A system which can let energy come in and go out, but not matter. For example, a battery, which gives electric power and can be recharged, but whose contents don't leak. Air is a closed system, as is your body.

Isolated System: A system that does not let energy or matter come in or go out. The Universe is an isolated system (since nothing can escape it or enter it); a sealed vacuum flask is another. Since our Universe is an isolated system, there are only finite amounts of matter and energy that exist. No new matter or energy can be created, but they can be converted from one form to another.

Work: In Physics, work means the conversion of any form of energy into mechanical kinetic energy, which moves a device.

Energy: It is defined as the force in Newtons required to move an object by one metre. The unit of energy is Newton-metre, also called Joule.

Heat Engine: A machine that converts heat energy (or any other kind of energy) into mechanical work.

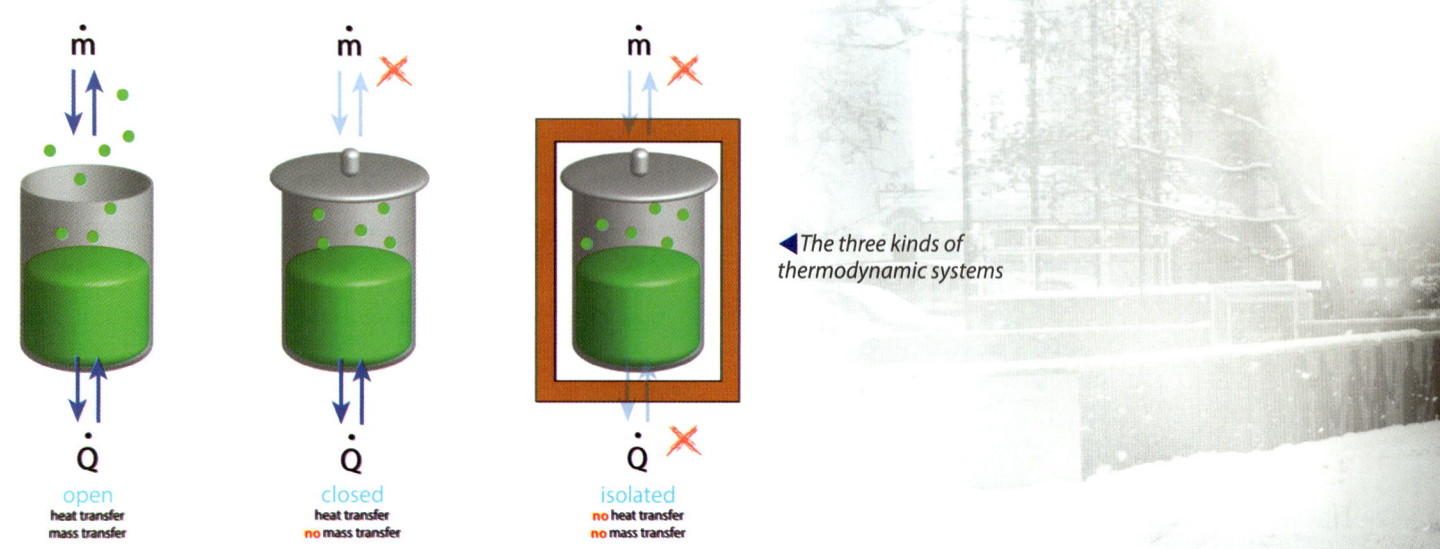

◄ *The three kinds of thermodynamic systems*

open
heat transfer
mass transfer

closed
heat transfer
no mass transfer

isolated
no heat transfer
no mass transfer

First Law of Thermodynamics

We've actually read this before as the Law of Conservation of Energy. In our practical world though, we think of the law in terms of using energy (symbol: Q) to drive work (W) in a machine. Some of that energy will remain unconverted and instead become part of the internal energy (ΔU) of the machine. Physicists show this in the form of an equation:

$$\Delta U = Q - W$$

A closed system that retains its internal energy is rare. Many engines give away the energy to the atmosphere in the form of waste energy. For a simple example, consider a kitchen blender making a smoothie. It converts incoming electric energy into the mechanical energy of the rotor blades. But some of the energy goes into heating the rotor blade. If you wash the blender immediately afterwards, the heat is lost.

▶ *Although thermodynamics was originally about heat engines, it can be applied to any kind of energy used to do work*

⊛ Incredible Individuals

You may have read that James Watt (1736–1819) was so fascinated by a kettle when he was a child that he went on to invent the steam engine. This story is not true. Watt did not invent the steam engine, but he did improve its design. He added a steam jacket that made sure that the heat of the engine was not lost; and a condenser that reduced the pressure of the steam, so that it would not make the engine explode.

◀ *James Watt's improved steam engines powered the Industrial Revolution*

▲ *A steam engine converts the thermal energy of compressed steam into the kinetic energy that makes the wheels move*

Second Law of Thermodynamics

According to the Second Law of Thermodynamics, an isolated system's entropy (the measure of molecular disorder of a system) will never decrease with time. When the forces between the atoms and molecules reduce, they have more freedom to move around, and the system becomes more random. For example, water left by itself will evaporate into the Universe. That is true even when the water is very cold, it will just be a lot slower.

Still, in many processes, this law does not really appear to hold. Otherwise, you would never get water to freeze—a process by which randomly floating liquid water molecules become arranged in a crystal of ice. But remember, when water is freezing, it has to lose heat to something else (usually air), which becomes more disordered in the process. Water and air together make the system.

▲ The Sun's entropy increases as it shines, and as it makes water evaporate, it makes the Earth's atmosphere's entropy rise too

Third Law of Thermodynamics

Entropy is the word used by scientists for the disorderliness of a system. It depends on the amount of pressure on the system, its temperature and other chemical properties. The Third Law says that if the temperature dropped to zero, such that there was no heat in the system at all, the entropy would also be zero. This is called Absolute Zero and physicists have worked it out to be -273.15°C. The system would become **infinitely ordered**, not just a solid, since even a solid's atoms or molecules have some freedom to vibrate. If this is hard to imagine, you're in good company; scientists have not yet achieved Absolute Zero practically, and cannot say what will happen at that temperature.

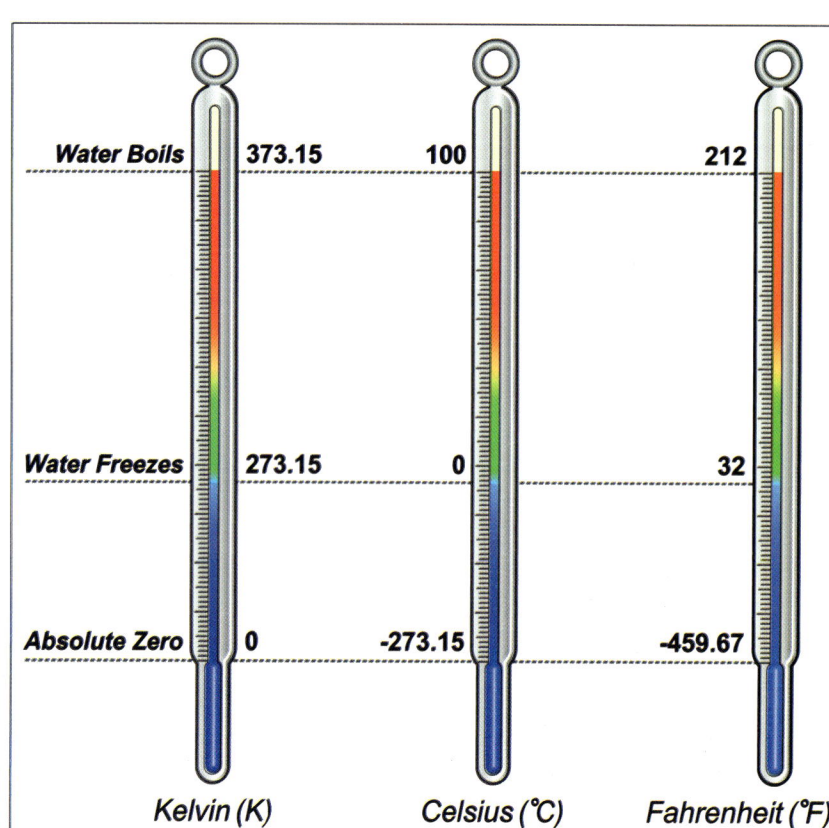

	Kelvin (K)	Celsius (°C)	Fahrenheit (°F)
Water Boils	373.15	100	212
Water Freezes	273.15	0	32
Absolute Zero	0	-273.15	-459.67

◀ At Absolute Zero, a system would freeze to infinite order, which no one has been able to achieve yet

👥 In Real Life

For long, humans have dreamt of the perfect machine, which works without needing any energy, or converts all the energy perfectly into work, which can then be converted back into energy. But the first kind of machine will violate the First Law of Thermodynamics, because any machine (including our bodies) needs energy to do work. The second kind of machine will violate the Second Law, because such perfect conversion is impossible.

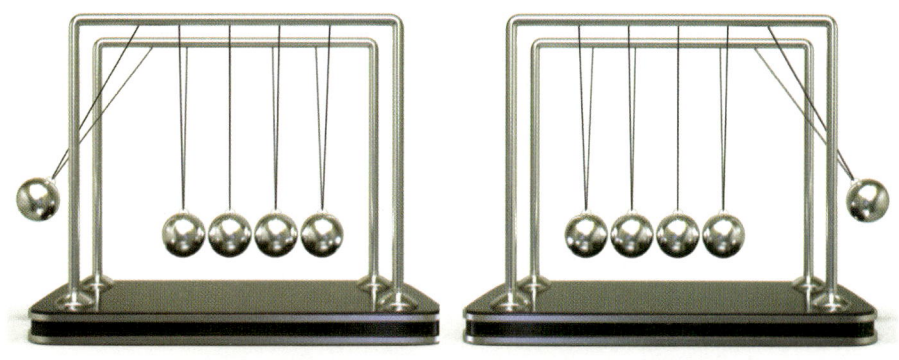

▲ *In theory, this would be a perpetual motion machine, as the energy of the first ball would make the last one move and rise. The last ball would then come down and in the same manner make the first ball rise again. But friction and gravity would soon bring the balls to rest instead of allowing continuous movement*

🔍 From Big Bang to Heat Death

According to the Second Law, the Universe should expand as it gets more disordered, and it does. According to the Third Law, at Absolute Zero, the Universe would have no entropy, so it would shrink to a point with no dimension (length, width, or height) at all. So, if the two are put together, we know how the Universe was born, and how it will die. The birth of the Universe is called the Big Bang. Its temperature was infinite, but its volume was zero. Therefore, it was infinitely dense. But since the Universe follows the Second Law, it began to expand very quickly as the temperature dropped, and it has been doing so for the last 13.8 billion years. What next? As it keeps expanding, the atoms and molecules will keep flying apart till the Universe becomes infinitely rare—so wide and deep and long that no atom would ever collide with another. Its entropy would become the maximum possible, but the Universe would have died. This is called a Heat Death. Lucky for us, it's billions of years away.

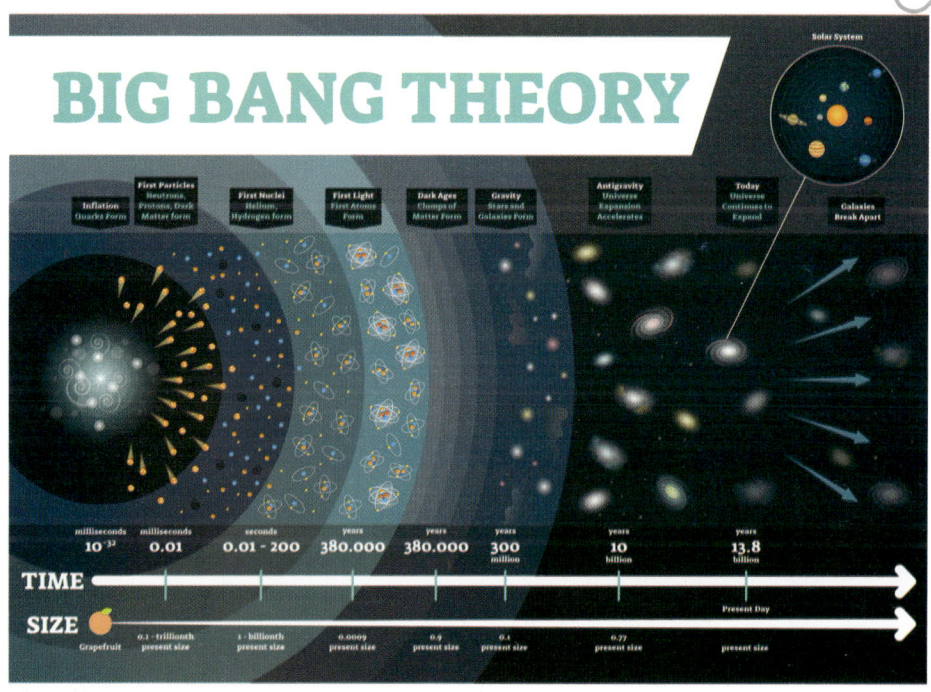

▲ *The birth and death of the Universe are based on the Laws of Thermodynamics*

⭐ Incredible Individuals

Anders Celsius (1701–1744) is most famous for inventing the scale used in thermometers, now known as the Celsius scale. He originally set 0 degree as the temperature at which water boils, and 100 degrees as the temperature at which it freezes. Carl Linnaeus reversed the scale to what it is today.

Colour Mixing & Colorimetry

Artists have long known that if you mix two colours, you get a third one. After Isaac Newton discovered that white light was made of different colours, two scientists, Thomas Young and Hermann Helmholtz developed the Trichromatic Colour Vision theory. They noticed that the human eye is most receptive to three colours—red, blue, and green. These are now called primary colours. The colours you get by mixing any two of these are called secondary colours; if you mix all three you get white. Since then, artists and engineers have worked on getting all the colours from these three, and today we have the science of **colour theory**.

Additive Mixing

Additive mixing of colours is used for light rays and transmitted colours. This is the principle that works in electronic screens, in your TV, computer, mobile phone, or gaming console. The screen is divided into millions of tiny pixels, each of which is made of three light-emitting diodes (LEDs), which emit red, green, or blue light when electricity passes through them. The digital signal that reaches each pixel of your screen tells it how much of the three colours to emit. For example, say a pixel is told to emit red and blue in equal proportions. The light waves of red and blue fall on the cone cells that are sensitive to those colours, and the brain reads the two signals together. You 'see' a magenta signal at that pixel. The other secondary colours are cyan (blue + green) and yellow (red + green). This is called RGB colour mixing.

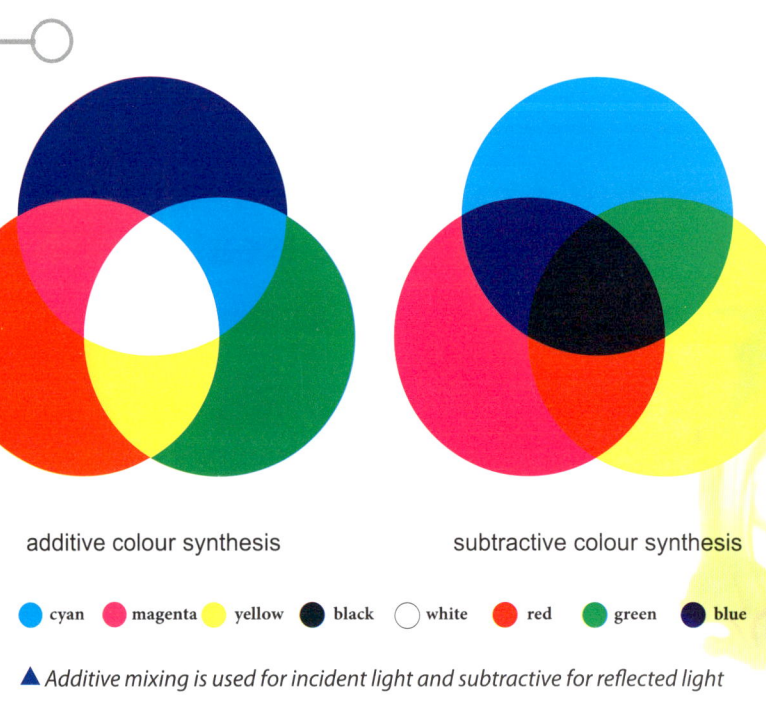

additive colour synthesis   subtractive colour synthesis

● cyan   ● magenta   ● yellow   ● black   ○ white   ● red   ● green   ● blue

▲ *Additive mixing is used for incident light and subtractive for reflected light*

👤 In Real Life

The colour wheel was invented by Isaac Newton to show how white light was made of different colours. If you rotate it really fast, the colours cancel each other out as they reach your eye, and you see a white disc. Newton's wheel uses red, blue, and yellow as the primary colours.

▶ *The colour opposite each primary colour is its complimentary colour*

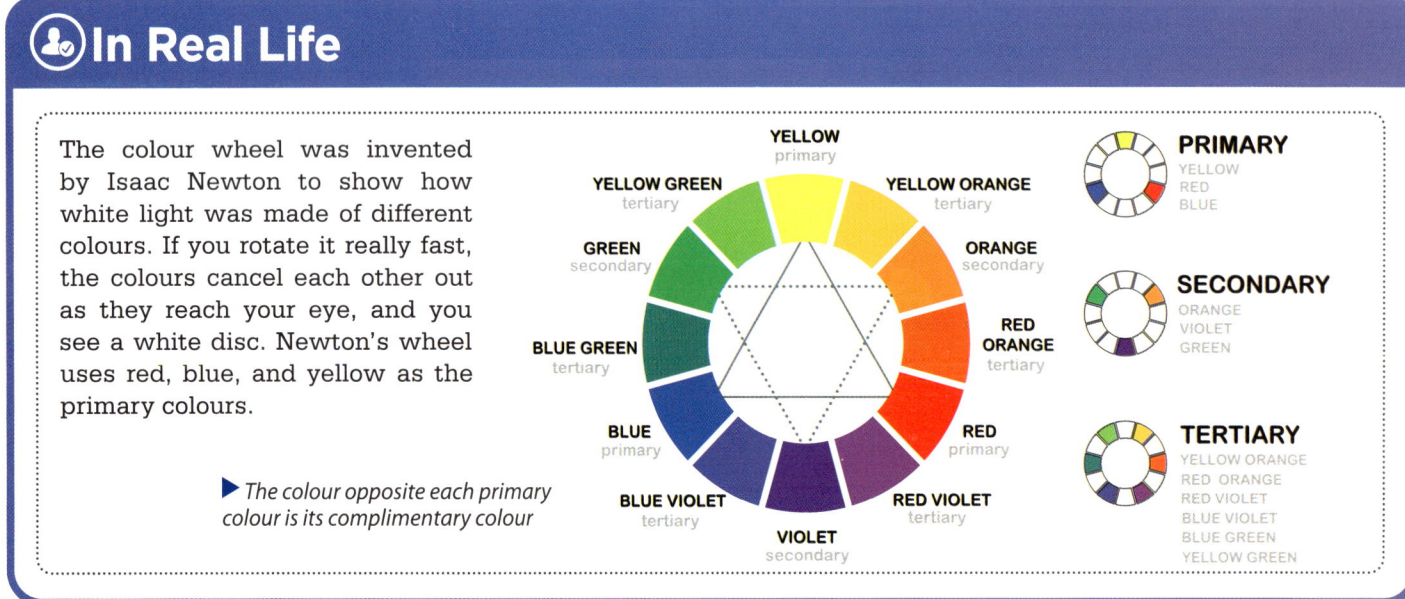

YELLOW
primary

YELLOW GREEN
tertiary

YELLOW ORANGE
tertiary

GREEN
secondary

ORANGE
secondary

BLUE GREEN
tertiary

RED ORANGE
tertiary

BLUE
primary

RED
primary

BLUE VIOLET
tertiary

RED VIOLET
tertiary

VIOLET
secondary

PRIMARY
YELLOW
RED
BLUE

SECONDARY
ORANGE
VIOLET
GREEN

TERTIARY
YELLOW ORANGE
RED ORANGE
RED VIOLET
BLUE VIOLET
BLUE GREEN
YELLOW GREEN

🔍 Subtractive Mixing

Additive mixing works only for incident light. If you mix the colours as paint though, you will end up with black! That's because paints and pigments are made of materials that absorb light of all wavelengths except the ones of their 'colour'. If you mix them, you end up with a mix that absorbs everything. Instead, like the artists and engineers who work in colour printing, you have to use a different scheme known as CMYK (cyan, magenta, yellow, and key). You mix pigments in such a way that the mix reflects only the colour you want. Here the primary and secondary colours of the RGB scheme switch places. If you print a picture with cyan and magenta in equal proportions, you get blue. CMYK, nevertheless, uses a black ink separately (called key), to get a darker shade.

▲ *Colour cartridges in printers have pigments that mix cyan, magenta, yellow, and black*

💡 Isn't It Amazing!

A number of studies have shown that male humans cannot distinguish as many colours as female humans. The wavelength also matters: men will see yellow where women see orange, and blue-green to women is blue to men.

▲ *How many shades of pink can you make out?*

Putting Light to Work

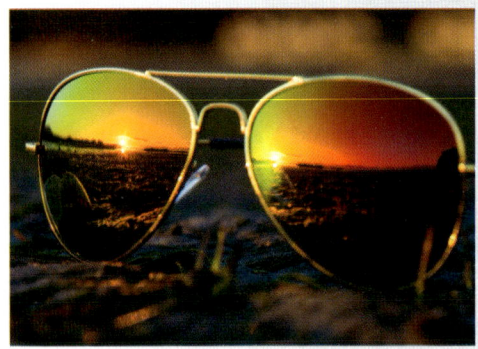

▲ *Polarized sunglasses have polarizing filters in them which reduce the amount of light entering your eyes*

When a light wave is moving, you know that the photons vibrate creating a magnetic field. But all the photons do not vibrate in the same direction. This is called unpolarised light. However, when light passes through some materials, only the photons that vibrate in a certain direction are transmitted and the rest are absorbed. This light is now called polarised light. It has many uses; one of them being in photography to get clearer pictures, by using a polaroid lens.

Colour Filters

A **colour filter** is a prism or a lens that reflects photons of certain wavelengths and transmits others. The atmosphere acts as a giant light filter, which filters out light of short wavelength. In the morning and evening, as the sunrays fall on us obliquely, the light has to pass through more air. The long wavelength photons (red-orange) pass but the blue ones don't, making the Sun look red.

Other filters are made of coloured glass and crystals for different uses. They help create a beam of light of almost a single wavelength (called monochrome light), which has many uses, especially in lasers. Light filters are used in spectrometry, fluorescence microscopy, and many other fields, often alongside a polarizing filter.

◄ *Colour filters are used to create monochromatic light*

Colorimetry

Colorimetry is a technique used by chemists to find out the concentration of a coloured substance in a solution. It works on the principle that the substance will transmit all the photons that match its colour and absorb the rest. If you use a light beam of a colour complimentary to the substance, the more amount of the substance there is, the more photons it will absorb. By measuring the intensity (number of photons per second) of the transmitted light, you can find out the amount of substance present in the solution. This is usually done by using a photovoltaic cell, in which the photons attack electrons and set off a small current.

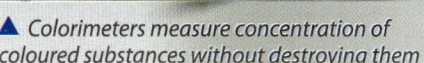

▲ *Colorimeters measure concentration of coloured substances without destroying them*

Lasers

Lasers were invented by Theodore Maiman (1927–2007) in 1960. A laser is a beam of monochrome, polarised light that has photons of very high energy. They are made by striking photons onto a charged material. The photons take up the energy of the electrons in the material, producing a stronger beam of light. By doing this repeatedly, the energy of the photons can be amplified to several thousand times.

The energy of a laser is enough to burn things, so lasers are used for cutting and welding materials very precisely, especially in the electronics industry. Lower-energy lasers are used to burn cancer cells and in surgery as very high-precision knives. LASIK surgery is an application of lasers used to reshape the cornea to improve vision, eliminating the need for glasses or contact lenses.

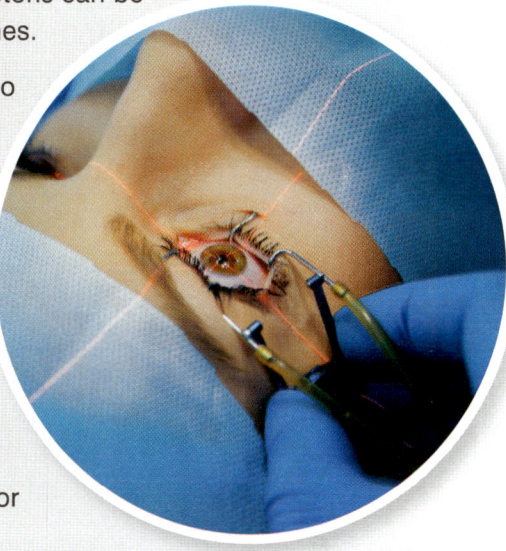

▲ *While LASIK technology is improving, there are enough risks involved with using lasers in the eye that make people cautious*

⭐ Incredible Individuals

Lasers are usually delivered in **pulses**, rather than continuous waves. A high-energy laser pulse could not be amplified beyond a point without damaging the equipment. Donna Strickland, a Canadian physicist, solved this problem. She reduced the energy but increased pulse time, and then amplified the pulse to high levels of energy. Finally, this high-energy pulse was reduced to a smaller-sized pulse of even higher energy. For this, she received the Nobel Prize in 2018.

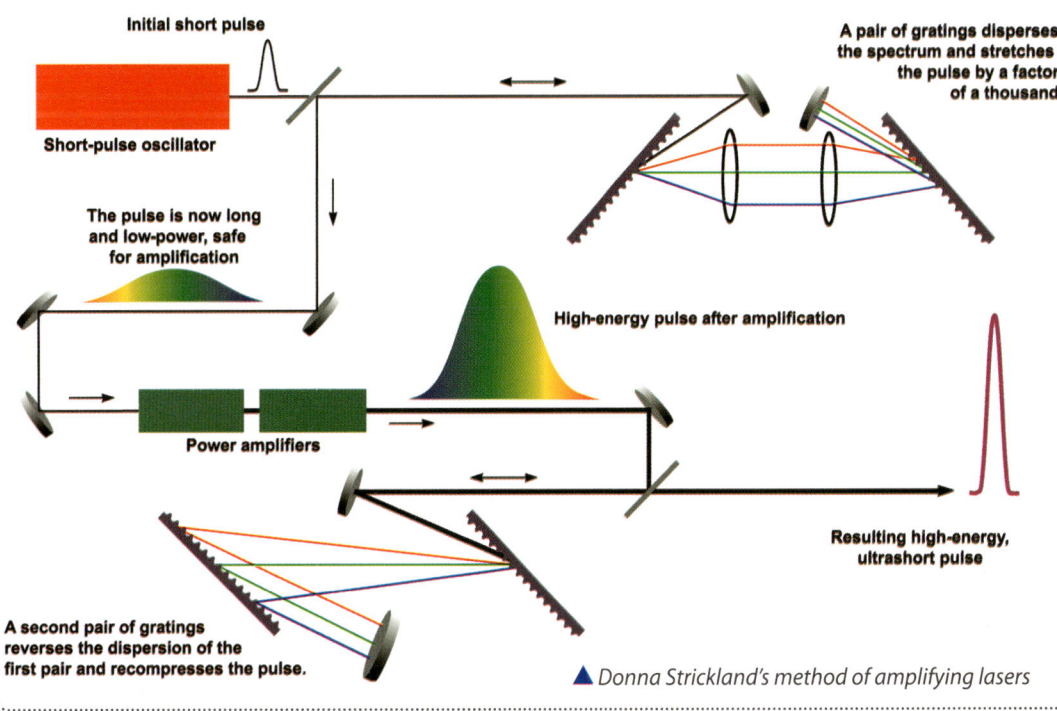

▲ *Donna Strickland's method of amplifying lasers*

Optical Illusions

An optical illusion is something that fools your eye into seeing something that isn't quite there. You would think this is only for conjurers and tricksters, but it is part of a huge industry that we love: the movies! Did you know that a '**motion picture**' is actually a giant visual illusion? That's because our eyes are digital in nature. They see the world in snapshots, with about twelve '**frames**' every second. If a series of still pictures run faster than that in front of our eyes, we think they are moving. Most motion pictures are shot at about 24 frames per second (FPS), so you see a smooth movement. Largely, they can be divided into three classes: physical, physiological, and cognitive illusions; with each having the 4 types discussed below.

▲ In the old days, a film projector would run 24 or more frames of a camera film over a concave lens to 'show' the film

🔍 Other Optical Illusions

Apart from the movies, the illusions we have fun with can be be classified into four types:

Ambiguities: These are illusions that make us see the same image in more than one way. The drawing of a cube is one: is it facing downwards or upwards? These illusions work by tricking the retinas of your eyes into seeing two different pictures, which the brain must then resolve.

Distortions: These make us see imaginary angles and curves. They make use of how the brain creates 3-dimensional (3D, also **stereoscopic**) vision by combining the images from the two eyes.

Paradoxes: These also fool our stereoscopic vision into seeing what is physically impossible. The artist M.C. Escher made many drawings of illusions like these.

Fictions: These make us see things when there aren't any. They make use of the fact that our brains don't record every detail of what we see, but only the boundaries between colours, and they mentally make up the rest.

Incredible Individuals

Charles-Émile Reynaud (1844–1918) was a painter, photographer, engineer, and industrial designer, who made one of the world's first animated movies. He invented the praxinoscope, the precursor to the modern projector. It had a series of pictures on a turntable; if you cranked it fast enough, you could see motion.

◄ *Reynaud's Praxinoscope works on the principle that the human eye sees more than 12 FPS as motion*

Isn't It Amazing!

Why do you need 3D glasses to watch a 3D movie? That's because they create an elaborate illusion of depth in a flat image. The movie is made of two separate images, that you can resolve only by separate cyan and red filters on your glasses. The two images reach your brain, where they are merged to form a 3D image.

ALPHABET
STEREO ANAG
3D LYPH
FONT DESIGN

ABCDEFGHIJKLMN
OPQRSTUVWXYZ
0123456789.?!

▲ *The two colour filters separate the two images, which reunite in the brain to form a 3D image*

🔍 Forced Perspective

Our eyes receive information about the world onto a flat surface (the retina). The brain has to figure out the distance of objects from this flat image, so it uses the relative sizes of images. Faraway objects look small because the brain is saying to itself that if it looks small when it should look bigger, it must be far. Some kinds of illusions make use of this. This is called forced perspective.

▼ *Is the castle really sitting on the birdbath?*

Isn't It Amazing!

Pareidolia is our brain's tendency to perceive a meaningful image in a random visual pattern. In the African Savanna where humans evolved, the ability to spot a lion's or an enemy's face in the grass meant life or death.

▲ *Do you see a double fire hydrant or a big-eyed face?*

Word Check

Biconvex Lens: A lens in which both surfaces are curved outwards, as in a magnifying glass

Chemical Energy: This is the energy stored in chemical bonds between atoms

Colour: The way your brain distinguishes each wavelength of visible light

Colour Blindness: The inability of some humans to distinguish light of certain wavelengths

Colour Theory: The theory that all colours can be derived by mixing the three primary colours

Combustion: The reaction of some substances with oxygen when they are heated

Concave Lens: A lens in which one or both surfaces are curved inwards

Convection Current: The circular movement of atoms or molecules in a liquid or gas caused by the heating of one side

Convex Lens: A lens in which one or both surfaces are curved outwards

Detector: An electronic device that creates a current when an electromagnetic wave falls on it

Efficiency: The ability of an engine to convert the maximum input energy into work

Electric Charge: A property of matter that makes it react to an electromagnetic field

Electromagnetic Energy: The energy of a moving electric charge or magnetic field

Electromagnetic Spectrum: The range of all wavelengths of photons, including gamma-rays, X-rays, ultraviolet light, visible light, infra-red waves, microwaves and radio waves

Frame: A single still picture in a motion picture reel

Freezing/Melting Point: The temperature at which a liquid becomes solid while losing energy, and a solid becomes liquid while gaining energy

Gamma Rays: Very high energy electromagnetic waves with wavelengths smaller than X-rays, emitted from nuclear reactions

Heat Energy: This is the energy stored in the movement of atoms

Image: The representation of an object formed by reflection from a mirror or refraction from a lens or prism

Infinite Order: The state of matter at Absolute Zero, where the atoms or molecules have zero freedom to vibrate

Infrared (IR) Waves: Low energy electromagnetic waves with wavelengths smaller than visible light but longer than microwaves

Ionising Radiation: Electronic waves that can remove electrons when they hit an atom and turn them into positively charged ions

Lens: A block of glass through which light is made to pass to refract it

Mechanical Energy: The energy that we see in the movement of objects

Mechanical Waves: Non-electromagnetic waves made by the movement of atoms and molecules

Melting: The phenomenon by which a solid becomes liquid

Microscope: A device to make a tiny thing look much larger than it is

Mirror: A surface that reflects light

Motion Picture: An optical illusion that tricks the eye into perceiving motion by showing still pictures at a very fast rate

Non-ionising Radiation: Electronic waves that cannot remove electrons when they hit an atom

Optical Magnification: The ratio of the size of an image to the size of the object creating it

Optical Resolution: The smallest distance between two objects that can make them appear as separate images through a lens

Periscope: A device to make an image of an object that cannot be seen directly

Power: A numerical value that indicates how far a person's eye's focal point is from their retina. Power zero indicates perfect vision

Pulse: An electromagnetic wave delivered for a very small period of time, used in radios and lasers

Quantised: The property of all energy to be made of tiny units called quanta

Radio Waves: Very low energy electromagnetic waves with wavelengths longer than microwaves

Stereoscopic or 3D Vision: The ability of the brain to perceive the depth of the image by combining the images of the retinas of both eyes

Subtractive or CMYK Colour Mixing: Obtaining reflected colours by mixing two or more secondary colours

Telescope: A device to magnify the image of an object that is very far away

Thermodynamics: The science of understanding how energy can be converted to work

Van der Waals Forces: Weak forces that hold the atoms or molecules of a substance together in liquid state

Wavelength: The distance a photon moves while completing a single vibration

X-rays: High energy electromagnetic waves with wavelengths smaller than ultraviolet light but more than gamma rays